T0365830

INFACTUHATED

*Poems of Love, Loss,
Lies, and Loathing*

PRESTON MOE

AuthorHouse™ LLC
1663 Liberty Drive
Bloomington, IN 47403
www.authorhouse.com
Phone: 1-800-839-8640

© 2014 Preston Moe. All rights reserved.

*No part of this book may be reproduced, stored in a retrieval system, or
transmitted by any means without the written permission of the author.*

Published by AuthorHouse: 03/06/2014

ISBN: 978-1-4918-7071-6 (sc)
ISBN: 978-1-4918-7070-9 (e)

*Any people depicted in stock imagery provided by Thinkstock are models,
and such images are being used for illustrative purposes only.
Certain stock imagery © Thinkstock.*

This book is printed on acid-free paper.

*Because of the dynamic nature of the Internet, any web addresses or links contained in this book may have changed
since publication and may no longer be valid. The views expressed in this work are solely those of the author and do not
necessarily reflect the views of the publisher, and the publisher hereby disclaims any responsibility for them.*

Dedicated to my friend JP

Gone but never forgotten

Tribute

The great road we all find ourselves on
Walking amongst each other atop the delicate dirt
It is where we arise, and tis where we perish
It is the foundation of life, strong
But life is fragile, just as soil crumbles under pressure
Its delicateness is what makes it beautiful,
How it is only held by a person for so long, before it fades away
But just as the dirt is carried on with the wind, life follows
Where it was once restricted, now it is infinite
When once vulnerable to despair, now stands invincible
Life is the path we walk, death is ultimately the destination
But just as one journey ends, another rises
For humans always tread in circles
The grief in our chests may slowly dissipate
But our love for you will be forever great

BELONG

Backwards I came, now I'm confronting
Besiege my thoughts, for they are haunting
Believing my life has some sort of purpose
Below my gods eyes I am worthless
Being lonesome has ceased to suffice
Belonging to something would sure feel nice

REGRET

Ravaging the once protected thoughts
Revenge of the broken truce once constructed
Regular torments of the vivid actions
Rejecting Grand opportunities in spite
Redeeming Gruesome acts committed
Regretting actions with no remorse

LINGER

Lonesome nights of continuous judgment
Littering the floor with horrific letters
Lining the virgin paper with vindictive words
Meddling in affairs beyond comprehension
Lying Engulfs words of wisdom
Lingering far beyond final words

PROMISE

Partake in the daily scrutiny
Practice the humility that is needed
Prosper with the morals freshly conceived
Prompt the vindictive stares of judgmental faces
Promote Independence and rise distinguished
Protect misguided decisions with dying effort
Promise that you wont succumb to adversity

DEATH

Dangerous attraction to Lucifer's knife
Devouring skin as it caresses the maimed flesh
Deafness as the final screech of depression expels
Dead Teenagers litter the graveyard
Death swarming fragile innocent ambitions

CORPSE

Calming words from the holy preacher
Confessions of sinner craving redemption
Corrosive tales of shameful past
Corporates businessmen with malicious obsession
Corrupted Psych preying on confidence
Corpse disgraced as lust subsides briefly

AGONY

Always saving the lonely soul
Against the villain with no self control
Fagot principles according to the chief
Antagonist for the suffering's grief
Agony for all who cant afford the toll

INSIDIOUS

Ideals of prosperity lost in mayhem
Incredible destruction fueling nightmares
Insomnia exhausting empathy of victims
Insistent words with malevolent content
Inside the head, overtaking conscience
Insight Divides paths open to wander
Inspect Idiotic principles of morality
Insincerely, Devious slander arises
Insidious pleasures controlling life

MEMORY

Mighty recollections of contentment
Menacing flashbacks constantly blitzing
Member's only admittance
Memoirs freshly scribed for privileged few
Memorizing instances of extreme consciousness
Memory resurrected to breath validity

CONFLICT

Cradling precious ideas with fragile love
Courageous smile through adversity
Continuously reassuring controversial decisions
Confronting antagonists with extreme prejudice
Confined Labyrinth of constant dismay
Confusing Lies deter oncoming support
Confessions with biblical consequences
Conflict dominating immanent encounters

IMPLY

Insane statements from Dictatorship accent
Immanent danger for ideas of treachery
Impossible salvation for sovereign thoughts
Imploding sense of morality
Implying government is legit

INFER

Image of the down civilian
Insanity ridden family outraged
Informed Politian's of mission success
Inferior enemy with tarnished religion
Inferring war on terror is necessary

BETRAY

Belittling the sacred words once preached
Believing diminishing respect will provide sanctuary
Bettering your self image in constant vain
Betrothing in attempt to conform another
Betraying as soon as chastity broken

DECEIT

Damaging words breaking confidence
Devilish smile as critical wounds become lethal
Decreased empathy with every skirmish
Descending into spiral of destruction
Deceiving eyes influence false trust
Deceit flowing through veins powered by corrupted heart

DETERMINED

Dictating every aspect of daily routine
Devouring any thought of free will
Detached from sanity, chaos overcomes pathetic self
Detention extending far past a just punishment
Deteriorating confidence as self-disgust engulfs
Deserved term of enjoyment cruelly interrupted desolation erodes memories once so treasured
Defiance promptly terminated with extreme prejudice
Deterred towards mines with malicious intent
Determined to live I revolt

DREAM

Deranged people once resorting to sleep to find serenity
Driven to insanity with constant emerging nightmares
Drenched in sweat as violent scream wakes self
Dreaded evenings as prolonged urges of rest overpower
Dreams, once a sanctuary have become hostile takeovers

OPIATE

Offering glimpse of relief as endorphins surge
Opposing all the threats that constantly bombard me
Opinions seeming irrelevant as mind attains unity
Operating as though apathy is the norm
Optimism attacked as high recedes
Opiate addicted for natural stimulation cant suffice

DISEASE

Daunting amount of obstacles to overcome
Dictating every aspect of your life
Disabled body
Paradise lost as reality sinks in
Disembarking on journey full of anguish
Disengaged as words of support fall unnoticed
Disease ridden, craving the end becomes inevitable

PANIC

Poor understanding of situation manifests into chaos
Passing judgment on victims as though defendants
Pandemic of colossal wreckage unfolding
Companions becoming severe opponents
Panic induced psychosis unravels reason

SECRET

Speaking in confusing riddles to disguise facts
Serving your own prerogatives with extreme loyalty
Secluded few with patience to overcome the manipulations
Wisecracks adverted to obtain latent truths
Secretions of anxiety are expelled from deceitful cells
Secrets exposed as hypocrite is revealed

TRUST

Towards the heart this feeling lurches
Traveling past my stomach, as observed by the fluttering butterflies
True emotions displace all doubt that once resided
The intrusive act of prying open my soul, so others can enter.
Trust in what feels right, for it is true?

PART 1—LOVE

3 Words

In the alphabet there are Twenty-six letters.

Living in harmony with ten numerical digits.

On the surface there's countless words to form, causing

Very few letters that form countless possibilities.

Employed by one to get a subtle point across,

Just so I can show you.

The numbers of ways you make me feel,

Multiplying by each growing second.

Making it harder and harder to fall asleep,

Without the thought of you circulating my mind.

There are only a few words that can explain it, and

You can search amongst the lines to find them.

Only 110 words were written here, when

Ultimately all I needed to say were 3.

Electricity

My feelings for you deeply lingers,

Within my heart, my soul but remains unseen.

The sensation spread throughout body, even through my fingers,

Transferring of static electricity as my hands explore your being.

Creating Goosebumps to rise, and a spike in heart beat,

You've convinced me the reality of love, no easy feat.

Now as I dream, I hear your whisper within my ear,

The sweet vibrations beat the drum, feeling as though you are here.

The ink on the page written dries as being scribed,

These lines cannot be erased, the feelings cannot hide.

Scenes in which I imagine amongst you have taken siege,

And these thoughts I do cherish, as you would believe.

Now as I caress my heads upon your fragile frame,

Causes a sudden rush of endorphins making me feel insane.

Silent small explosions of firing neurons within my skull,

Causing me to think the future with you will never be dull.

Read this now, feel as though I am beside you on that cold winter table,

And know that I sometimes try to not think of you. But am unable.

Have you?

Have you ever wondered about who you are?

Have you ever wished for happiness under a shooting star?

Have you ever looked in the mirror and ask, "Who am I"?

Have you ever questioned if anyone would care if you die?

Have you ever seen someone stare at you for some while?

Have you ever you ever asked yourself "why" when you see someone smile?

Have you ever listened to yourself when your conscience says something real?

Have you ever glanced at someone and realize how they feel?

Have you ever tried so hard to keep your feelings at bay?

Have you ever talked to someone who seems to make your day?

Have you ever seen something that changed your mind?

And have you ever looked for something you could never find?

M.I.A

Every time I leave it hurts more

Knowing that I will one day be back

Feeling as though I left for war

As my heart is constantly under attack

Loving every second I'm here

Dreading all the time I am alone

Overcome by the sense of fear

Craving the day I come home

Love hurts, for it leaves you open

But its something I'll always put hope in

I could write 100 lines to this poem

But it wouldn't quite suffice

Cause without love I have no home

And without you I have no life

Life

Hanging ideas tied to the birch branch.

Beside the swing that so many great memories were based upon.

Flashbacks vividly relived all during a glance.

Having to realize that the future is bleak, and the past is gone.

Death? That is the only thing that is a guarantee in ones time on earth.

Life? Even though promised for a while, always slips away.

These are the obstacles we are faced with from the day of birth.

And the resulting heartaches till our final day

Chemistry of Life

The stimulation within my stomach has ceased to occur.

There is no chaotic uncontrolled fluttering of insects.

Butterflies evolved to mosquitoes, to become no see em, became no feel em.

My soul is an atom of carbon, organic, vast, but empty.

There is a nucleus at the center, but a cloud of nothingness surrounds it.

The electrons don't move around here adjoined, they be as Bohr predicted.

No probability of them interacting upon each other to create energy. No sign of life.

However, it is not dead, it is unreactive.

It is a quadruple bonded Carbon, It is content with itself.

All I am is a Carbon after all. 6 protons, 6 electrons. But empty.

I crave electrons, to be with another to fill up my base pairs.

Someone to control my electronegative ways.

I am also oxygen, but oxygen supports life, I feel none inside me.

Someone to hear me rant about the importance of this incredible element.

You are Xenon. Perfect. But unable to bond with this Carbon.

I am merely another wannabe, wanting to fill my orbitals as you did.

We can be bonded for an instance, but the repulsion forces us apart.

Carbon is everywhere it seems; it is the backbone of life.

It is constantly being used to form molecules in which it has no say, consuming energy.

I am Carbon. Butterflies are Carbon. We are there to be used.

My bound is infinite, I am nothing.

I am Chemistry.

Direction

When I first laid my eyes on your face

Your beauty stopped me, locking me in one place

Since then, I have never lost that initial feeling of your beauteous charm

I dedicated my life to never letting you be harmed

When I fall asleep with your face circulating in my mind

These experiences are so powerful and divine and are only mine

Trust and loyalty will always be shown with you

The thought of anyone else just won't do

You're the North Star keeping me in the right direction

Even that star is jealous of your beauty and perfection

So read this to feel safe and protected

For I will never let your need become neglected

Lonely Day for a Coward

There I see the girl by the corner

Should I introduce myself or just ignore her

I walk past with my head hung from a lack of courage

Scared of what I would say and the resulting damage

She seems to be quiet and mysterious

But that makes all the more curious

Just to talk to her would be a reward

One that is unachievable by this coward

How do two people meet and grow close

When a rare smile is all that is shared, at most

Nothing good will come of this I assume

So I will just retreat from the impending doom

Careless Beauty

Beauty stands before both guilty and innocent

To be in the presence is a feeling that is heaven sent

Beauty is not bias or prejudice to the observer

So extraordinary that is should only be given to proper deservers

Beauty can be found between everything and everyone

When it is revealed it is an event in which the spectator has won

From a simple flower to a complex individual

People always attempting to make it a daily ritual

Brain losses thought, heart skips a beat, body becomes motionless

All my senses are trying to allow your beauty to be harnessed

Finally in your eyes I am able to see life's secluded treasures

Ones not of wealth and possession but of simple pleasures

How can one be so fortunate to see your elegance in a day?

One would be willing to sacrifice sense and sanity to never let it fade

In your presence I am both completely liberated and entirely enslaved

Blissful

Cursed and Blessed

When love and betrayal are assessed

Scared and tormented

When jealously blocks me from hearing what's said

Anger and ignorance

When my fists clinched and I begin the infection of sin

Regret and remorse

When my bloodied hands remind me of my unforgivable course

How will God judge me on that final day?

After I am buried beneath that sky of gray

Will he see my deeds or acknowledge my wrongs?

Will I be sent to hell or be blessed with angels songs?

If I am found, guilty I will accept my consequence

For after losing you, I could never fill the absence

The Fight

To fight for love is not a battle of fists

Nor is it a battle of wits

It's a surrender of conflict and self

Sacrificing time, friends and health

The three words those are deadly

And often used unreadily

When it's forced, it hides

When not attained, it cries

Giving something for everything

Showing this promise with a wedding ring

Love is here and it truly exists

Bound tightly around my wrists

PART 2—HUMANITY/ NATURE

Milk Carton Love Story

Have you heard about?

The girl who was discarded in the forest,

Left to decay without hope.

Oh, I need to further mention,

The man who forgot all the morals he learnt,

And never bothered to discover em again.

Now, I can't forget,

The mother who cried, as her child never came home,

To kiss her goodnight and swarm her in love.

Unfortunately I have to say,

The world forgot about that girl, she was just a phase,

forgotten and replaced in a few short days.

What If?

What if the world was full of prosperity and truce?

What if the world wasn't tightening its own noose?

What if people chose integrity instead of greed?

What if everyone received what they need?

What if it was easier to talk than fire a weapon?

What if the world became a heaven?

What if the rich didn't condemn the poor?

What if democracy overpowered war?

What if one day the pain will cease?

What if the world was enveloped with peace?

This day, the day of peace and knowledge will never occur

For our lust for power and wealth will always block this door

Ruined—Preston Moe

Where has the peace gone?

When all that we do is drop bombs

Where has the love disappeared?

When all the kindness in the world is covered in fear

Why don't the underprivileged take a stand?

When appreciation is all they demand

Why do people say that slavery is extinct?

When young children are forced to work, forbidden to think

Why are governments so corrupt?

Killing innocent people for a quick buck

Why is the world beyond salvation?

When the ones that destroyed her are her own creation

Conflict

Abandoned, he turns away from the night

Crawling from fear, begging for light

Hearing him squirm, him pleading for aid

Screaming sounds from someone who's never afraid

This is only a tragedy

The stalker screeches to infer dear

No time to run, it's already here

Cant deny it any longer, its time for conflict

One will leave a victim, the other a convict

The being caresses the shoulder

The grip is tight, can't be broken

With every constriction, the chills get colder

With every cry, the man loses hope in

The future, his past, what he had to do

But for the remorse he feels, he'll feel that before it's through

Destructive Beauty

There's a reason why it's impossible to stare at the sun,

why we aren't allowed to gaze upon its beautiful radiance,

As its descendants we are unworthy to observe its raw power,

But instead, we can only gander atop the ground as though servants.

It warms us, provides us with energy and sustenance,

And we should be thankful for its merciful donation.

However, the sun will one day destroy us,

Even now it warns us of its destructions as its radioactive rays deteriorate our very flesh

From ashes we raised, and to ashes we will descend.

The suns gracious sense of control prohibits it from reclaiming us as fuel,

But one day, its cravings will overcome its gravitational force

As humans, we may look upon an ant with a feeling of empathy, halting our step

But we as humans do not look upon something we cant see with the same prejudice

Do we feel a sense of remorse as we break apart a uranium atom?

Changing what it once was. Abusing its chemical structure for a glimpse of energy?

To the sun, we are invisible; we are only a conglomerate of molecules

We are composed of the universes most explosive elements,

Even though proclaim ourselves as individuals, when we are only hydrogen, carbon and oxygen

We are the suns gas station on its last hope for arriving to a destination.

Running on empty it will reap us of our components as it engulfs us in a supernova

Looking at each other with disgust for color or race, when the fact is that we will all burn the same color.

So remember its better not to agitate the sun, so don't dare look at it.

For it will only bring tears to your eyes.

The World

The sky swarmed with birds flying
So gracefully, diving and crying
The eye of god looks through the sun
Seeing the horrible deeds we have done
Our technology has formed into a knife
Used to kill and cut down on life
Even though one can't see the future ahead
Without intervention, we will be dead
Even though humans have perished
The world now will flourish
For our parasitic ways have ceased
The world tries to survive our disease
For if humans do not begin to learn
Our cancer will certainly burn
The world

Wake me up when the war ends

Awake me when the war had dispersed

This eternal sleep has no end

This battle has shown the cruelty of man and worse

Killing the enemy and ultimately your own friend

In war the dead are the only ones that see peace

Flag lowered to honor the lost and deceased

The soldiers are praying for the end of horror

Only thing present is blood and gore

Morality of man had seemed to disappear through the cracks

Podium stands are being replaced with gun racks

Voices are drowned in the chaos of gunfire

Lives are being sold and distributed to the highest buyer

Take a stand and rebel against the warlord

And live your life to your own accord

ARMY

Shaved heads, leather boots
Men and woman, young recruits
New life, without identity
Ready to fight for humanity
Weapons of fate with deadly powers
Revenging the fall of two towers
Relentless punishment towards the foe
No surrender. No flags painted as snow
Pride and honor stitched to their sleeves
Ridding the world of its disease
The good, the bad
The ecstatic and the sad
All the same in death
Leaving loves ones with nothing left

Audience for All

The final stroll of the unforgiving dead man
While glaring down at his guilty hands
What pain they have brought
All unconsciously and without thought
Morals have long so escaped
Broken, just as the victims he's raped
On that chair, full with charge
Ego now so small, when once so large
Spectators look down on him with utter disgrace
Watching as pleasure overcomes his face
A man who went wrong so many years ago
Will now perish in a way, resembling a freak show

Daily Life

Settle Down! Ordered

The teacher.

With a frown. Obeyed

The pupils.

Let us pray? Demonstrated

The preacher.

Not Today, Replied

The people.

Bring us peace! Pleaded

The dying.

Your life is on lease. Answered

The coroner.

Have some values. Asked

The crying.

They have no use. Dismissed

The governor.

No hope for tomorrow. Cried

The weak

Here's money you can borrow. Smirked

The Sheik

The nature rewritten

The mushroom grows not in a paradise
It's no flower, dependent on love
No one appreciates the simple grace of it
Persevering through damp mossy ground
Hidden from light, overcome by shade
It has no pretty effects, no pedals of red
But it does a purpose, which a flower incapable
It's a worker, a subject with a task
Renewing the earth, for it is its destiny
Thought the flower may rest upon valentines bed
The mushroom hides alone, amongst the dead
With no credit, no metaphors in its favor
But the mushroom goes on, in the dark
But if everything were lost, no rose no orchid would arise
Only the despicable shroom, would finally catch your eyes

Winter hell.

Molten slivers of sky dropping onto bare skin,

Tingling as the components are diluted into pores.

Fragrance of blooming weeds distant memory.

White walls of torment entrap the constant route,

Littered in waste as to reveal our once clean slate.

Condensation freezing as breath escapes crude words.

Compressed beauty collapses and shifts to wretched steel,

Transparent glass that tricks the mind of true ground.

Taking advantage of naive on comer.

The juncture of extended blindness.

Weakened radiation falls hopelessly on blank canvas,

Retreating in shame, overtaken by opaque obscurity.

Fueling the ideas of calamity

Paradise Pending

The islands came from nothing

Dirt and dust, emerged from Poseidon

From Africa we arrived, became something

World became ours, in an act of random

Destroyed what took so long to perfect

Left the future asking what now to dissect

Butchered to ground, the soil and the drink

Leaving the discards to slowly sink

Garbage left in the playground of nature

The ones once so free now trapped in danger

The ice melts leaving water to rise

The shoreline children playing, soon will hear cries

Their house be gone, their lives changed

People lose control, become deranged

Fight for a right, the right to feed

But the suns so hot, it burns the seed

The future seems distraught, now it's time to pray

For we will be die like the dinosaurs, but in a different way

No More!

War brought me here, to this dreadful haven
With men I trust, and a cause I've lose faith in
Fields planted with foes, friends and feeding crows
Revealing destruction of man, and the pain that follows
Once soldiers, respected. Now mercenaries, dishonored.
Fighting for pay, rights of man could not be bothered
Blindness handicaps me, in the brightness of sun
My bloodied hands, evidence of the horror I've done
Children were massacred, taken from orders
All for governments, fighting over boarders
Now as I speak, I begin to weep
For war murders everything, even sleep

Black Lights

Prolonged silences arise from darkened canvas
Intoxicated stars fall from their solitude positions
Explosions of light before destructive end
Magnetism dancing, craving attention
Skipping across the vacant ballroom
Light reflected, illumination the dull terrain
Foreshadowing the triumphant return
Diamonds shining, radiation so ancient
Possibly screaming their final dying words
Billions of years in travel, often never heard

Closing Time

I feel the end coming for the last time

See it hit the horizon for the blind

Shadows overtaking the earth we stand

Rivers fading away into barren sand

One more day is all that's allowed

Before the earth is consumed in vicious cloud

Lean your ear towards the dying earth

As she silently screams awaiting her rebirth

One that flourishes, one that succeeds

As our righteous death prospers the seed

PART 3—LIES

Dreams

When I fall, I quietly I wander through my dreams

I'm conscious to an extent, but unaware that what is happening is ridiculous

It feels so real, past memories intertwined with future events

Horrid memories in which I attempted to eradicate come back for revenge

They bombard me relentlessly, constantly bringing up something I've hidden

Through the weed grass I wonder, it rose above my line of sight

I navigate through the maize with my hands, spreading it as though a beaded door

The maze has grown from ideas that I've once planted in the cognitive soil

Ideas that have been derived from experience, what I should have done?

Consequently sprouting into dominant sporophytes, blocking me from seeing around the corner

The only direction I can manage is the sudden glimpse into the sky

Gaze amongst the stars trying to remember which one is true north

I was told that it's the brightest in the dark, the one that catches your eye

But they all seem bright, and are all deceiving in what they are trying to tell me

Abandoned

Abandon all ships! We are falling into the sea
Being dragged into the anaerobic doom beneath our feet
Feel Poseidon wraith as he pulls you towards ground below
With no sign of life from the loves ones, no glimpse of hope
Crippled from fear, chaotic breaths escape from my mouth
Whisper prays to some god, but they are whispers of doubt
Little by little the water reaches my position
The sharp chill of it hitting my ankle surprises me to clench my fists
I am going under, my life in shambles; sin about to be washed clean
Frozen in the water, as the last man dying is left to wonder
What could have been altered to change this outcome?

Redemption

Related to something once preached about in the Bible
Even though those powerful words seem redundant today
Demanding us to praise god as our savior
Evolutionarily beliefs have out grown our story
Making a collection of pages to be only an impressive novel
Printing money every time the name Jesus is inked
Though supposedly nonprofit, the church is a business
Identified as saints, but steal your wallet as you kneel to pray
Optimistic thoughts of serenity for internal time
Not once thinking of how ridiculous it sounds

Understanding

Time is getting run down, the clock is slowing

Individual attempts at salvation are left paused in progress

Even when I do my best to hide, my emotions are still showing

Without rescue I cannot triumph the raids, they attack my weakness

Just lend me a hand, one to hold when I feel the shivers overcome

Let me squeeze it when I'm scared, and when I feel numb

Tampering with fate is futile

Life ceases to be altered for an instance

Even rain attempts an attack on the cement only for a while

Looking at the past at only a passing glance

When god created man, he did not imagine what was in store

And when he rested on that seventh day, the world was already in war

Trying to devise a perfect world, but in that we eradicate the flaws

The individuals that had words within their hearts, were forced to shut their jaws

I have once prayed, for the well being of the ones I love

My prayers went unanswered, and I went on to curse the Gods above

We believe that this is how it works, pray and be answered

We've already lost hope in god, as we spread the streets with his filth

Whores, drugs and businessmen, throwing morals in the trash bin

Creating a vortex of despair, in which we get caught in

Having nothing left to choose from, they said this would happen

The judgment day will arise, we will pay for our sin

As god chooses who is righteous and who has wronged

We will finally know where we rightfully belong

The rapists, and thieves amongst the leaders of today

The ones that were cruel, the ones that betrayed the night, to see the day

They did it because the bible said

Only the religious will be loved, and the infidels are to be dead

This is what they interpreted, when reading that sacred ink

Stealing away peoples futures, without even the care to think

What is this?

The day is unrecognizable through my eyes
Disappointed that I believed all the lies
Now with less than nothing I pray
I pray that the gods end my pain with the end of day
The gods however never listens to my pleads
For I am guilty from my unforgivable deeds
Punished for letting you go without fighting
Reminded everyday by my continuous hiding
In adversity I can find redemption
Now the past is gone and never to be mentioned
Future is near and the present won't last
Letting my memories fall with the opening of my grasp
I realize now that being broken was a reward
For it caused me to grow and cease being a coward
This is what it is

Admittance

White wooden doors
Stained glass art
Behind it is horror
Behind it is dark
Alter with alter wine
Water with holy powers
Faith in religion is crime
Faith in God is sour
Death is around the corner
Lurking for its turn
Waiting for a stranded loner
Waiting to watch you burn
Hear me now as I reminisce
About life and what I miss
It's you that I crave
Torturing me from beyond the grave

Todays Lesson

Hear the song of angels sing.

Concentrate on the morals learned.

Have optimism like the sight of new spring.

Don't rush through life, respect your turn.

Cherish the memories, and evolve from em'

Stride for your passion, don't ever pause.

Beware of temptation, and her ferocious venom.

Be a man of honor, and support your cause

Never lose faith for its all we own

Avoid being timid, for what we experience is all we've known

And when pain stricken you, remember you're only a man

Hopelessness

Sunday mornings all built into our ritual of life

Beliefs being driven into you as though a knife

The bible explains how we've all wronged

But in modern day, the bible doesn't belong

Why listen to words that are from so long in the past

When the future is now, and it will hardly last

God is an idea in which I'm not completely sold

So my will goes against what it's been told

Bleeding sorrow out of the pores of humanity

Being driven crazy past the point of insanity

Listening to preaching men talk about lost truths

Having to repent my sins in a closed off booths

I will stand up, choose freedom and yell

Cause there's worse things than hell

Where to Begin?

The excruciating penetration of the blessed nails,
Tearing the flesh away from the scapegoat's skin.
The wooden cross in which he impales,
Attempting to save a nation from their unforgiving sin.

Erect the son, so God can witness his pain
Screaming mercy in agony, but in hell he will remain.
Mary's bastard son, who conceived with a god,
Proclaimed to be gods son, but seen as a fraud

Delivered to earth to be abused and killed,
A worthy sacrifice in which a religion began to build
The story forged into paper, with words that inspires
Even if the people preaching are liars

Resurrected, free now from stricken torment
Alive again, betrayed but free from resent.
Fade away, from dust to dust you will remain,
But your sacrifice will not be in vain

Walking Distance

The ground sinks, walls collapse, skies falls

Walking down gods never-ending halls

A maze of choices, a prison of regrets

Being imprisoned by what I wasn't able to get

My goals unfinished, my targets not reached

All these life lessons that I wasn't preached

I do not blame my upbringing for what I have become

Nor do I blame myself for what I have done

We have all sinned, but are all innocent in gods eye

But why follow someone's rule, when it all could be a lie

So why be good to humanity, when society is a fake

It is just better to live your life, and live it without hate

Redemption

An angel called to warn me of my awaiting sins

Have I wronged, or just been able to let my life begin

My god threatened me of horror if I continue my present path

But is that justifying being afraid of someone's wraith?

My soul tells me to continue doing what I think

But my mind is so timid it forbids me to blink

Open eyes are now able to see the horrid things I have created

Now it's my duty to, my purpose, to allow them to be eradicated

If love is glory, then what results from it must be glorious

Then why is this guilt inside me so torturous

My knees are bloodied from the praying to find redemption

However the constant battle of feeling is one I don't mention

I have been weighed, I have been measured, and I have been found wanting

For this reality is one that is forever haunting

PART 4—SADNESS / LOATHE

Hell

Sent to hell, and I met the devil.

Came from bad, trying to get better.

Living like a sinner, with memories I repress.

Went to church once, but I forgot to confess.

Been to hell, now I'm friends with the devil.

Cause lets be honest, I'm no angel.

Saw me fall once, now I back running

But don't get close, cause I'm not loving

Seen the pain that only happens once

And the lies spilt from mouths of these cunts

Get away from me, cause you haven't seen nothing

You're a two-face bitch, you need to stop fronting

Now I'm back from hell, and its only getting better

The only thing I'm leaving behind is this suicide letter

Cause I'm just a person living in fear

And when I go back to hell, imma stay there

Cause I've been to hell, and the devil was a friend

And he saw my pain and offered me an end

Now blood flows down and arm get redder

And my eyes are only getting wetter

I'm going back to hell with this final scream

Eyes close shut, and I begin to dream

Now going back to hell, here comes the light

I didn't give up; I'm just done the fight

Grief

Brittle glass shatters to heart shaped crystals against the granite tile

Crying with a tear stained face as I realize I will never again see your smile

Tears behaving as hail as they bombard the desk by which I write

Drowning my words in sorrow, night after night

The ink fades away as water erodes them from the page

But the feelings associated are ingrown, submersed below the rage

Cannot allow them to flee, they are mine to bare

And asking for help would not suffice, for not many would care

Even though aching, my fragile hand continues to scribble

Sensing though my soul is being eaten, nibble-by-nibble

But then again, did I even have much of one to begin?

As I've been feeling it fade, with every days end

The idea of heaven excites me, to see your smile again

I count down the days to reunite, my long lost friend

Companion

Watch it fall. On the vows you swore to protect.

See it spread. As it rapidly begins to infect.

By the darkest corner it grows to size

Lurking behind your back waiting for your demise

Ignore it as though it has wandered astray

But it's forever with you. Day after day

When you cease to exist it'll be done

It's job is over. It has won

Constantly with you. Till ground touches flesh.

The demon inside. Forever obsessed

The End

Will you bury me below that tree when I go?

Will you leave my grave unmarked so no one will know?

Will you scream at the top of your lungs for why did I leave?

As the fragile dirt crumbles beneath your knees

Can you let go of me as I fall deep?

And lower me down to my eternal sleep

Showing up to the grave to show me love

As you place down the flowers above

How will you handle the thought of losing me?

As I become only a fading memory

Will you remember me when you cease to rest?

And will you forget my bad, and only see the best

Can you let go of me as I begin to leave?

And realized now that your love is now deceased

Showing up to the grave to give me some care

As you continue holding on to pain too great to bare

See me now as my veins fail to pulsate

And realize now that I'm closer to that final date

Bringing me peace to a life of pain

And I will see victory, for I will be spared the blame

I will carry on through the light when I fall

And I will see my god as I enter his crowded hall

I will let him know that I have come in sorrow

And that my peers have live without me tomorrow

Can you lay me down beneath the tears you weep?

And sing a song of solitude for the weak

Can you lullaby me as you would if I was in womb?

Just now submersed by dirt in my eternal tomb

Imagination

Premonition of a horrific event to occur
Assuming it has something to do with her
Interpreting my surroundings as an attempt to see
Nevertheless seeing the antagonist is me
Forgetting something I discarded amongst the garbage
Undetermined if it's worth the effort to salvage
Lying to myself, to predict that the future is sure

Tomorrow I will return to my life as a drone
Having lose morality and unable to think on own
Owing my religion all I earned and possess
Ultimately losing all self worth as I become obsessed
Giving into orders, as rebellion seems futile
Harnessing love, but seeing no one worth the while
Trading anything to have an opportunity at redemption
Slowly realizing I have lost the war, through depression

Conflict

Every day is a battle, every morning a declaration of war

Removing yourself from your bounds is a subtle act of suicide

There is a light, one that blinds; it's outside your door

Sensational feeling of risk and fear, and you feel you almost died

Moon like footprints as you disturb a new path

Abstract objects around your peripheral, the ignorant innocents beside

We feel as though we have control over our life, when we don't hath

All these words of courage preached, there we were laid

Opening countless entrances, new areas able to explore

Having to understand, the wrong decision will cause disaster to occur

Scared of change, to my house once again I will reside

Secure in my room, unable to hide

Heartache

Memories that resurface after a period of solitude

Memories I tried to repress

Thoughts of goals I never accomplished to do

Thoughts that needed to be confessed

Imaginations that I have ceased to create

Imaginations that have surpassed their due date

Expired now, they become redundant today

With every word you scream at me, its one less I'm allowed to say

The dreams I once had of you were once to great to number

It was once a paradise, an escape to see you while I slumber

Excitements replaced by an empty feeling of anxiety of what's to become

We had our life set in stone, but my feelings became numb

Left me stranded with my dreams dead in hand

The once impeccable stone had disintegrated into sand

Mistakes educate, but there's a capacity of what can be learnt

My heart reached its payload, saying you were remorseful, but I knew you weren't

Bully

Remind us how to feel, the acceptance within our hearts

Dropping our kids off at a school, filled with hate from the start

We are our parent's children, for their beliefs are drilling into our heads

Let them be eradicated from our midst, let us choose instead

"Can I play with you guys?" but no one answers the boy

He is peculiar and unfit to have fun with the others

Hasn't he learned that he is garbage, just like his mother?

The kid's come around with sticks in hand, "they call him fag" and beat him down

He is being included at last in a game he dun understand

But the game is of hate, and redemption he will demand

Left him on the ground, with sand drenched in blood.

The kids have gone too far, what have they become

What has happened is evil, cannot be undone

Hatred of the kids, their parents to come

To save them from detention, cause they are good kids just young

Like their fathers n mothers, they make an excuse

That kids is a fag, he deserved that abuse

What ever happened to the good old days?

When women had no right, and we killed gays

Something must have happened to make this world change,

Probably that mother Teresa and the words she sprang

That beaten kid grew up, bruised but unbroken

The one called a fag, has married, and has put hope in.

A cause, a way to live and not succumb to a knife

Survive a suicide attempt, one that failed to end their life

Dark thoughts resume to spread

All he wishes is to be dead

But the look in his mothers eye as he awakes in intensive care

Prevents him from ever looking at deaths face again and accepting the dare

Go back home, to this place of solitude

And reminds themselves that the world is crude

Today's Notion

Today's notion

Depressed emotions

Dead thoughts

Happiness unable to be bought

Here alone in front of the fires

Being driven insane by my wanting desires

Throw it up and watch it fall

Bend down and begin to crawl

To the end and the final destination

Find the death in your own creation

Life filled with sorrow

Find hope in tomorrow

Drive

Blinding Lights
Across the road, the sky
Is this God? Is this a sign?
Has it come, is it my time?
Shrieking cries
In my ears, my head
What has happened, am I dead?
Lying face down, on the solid tar
Glass shattered, destroyed car
Open gate, Light ahead
I awake, in my bed.

Humanity vs. humility

Walk step by step unaware

Trudging past allies covered with dark

Craving life without a care

But overcome with pain in my heart

The watch on my wrist ticks by with leisure

One tick. Two Tick. Three is torture!

My mind is frozen, my body in seizure

Memories bearing overhead as though a vulture

Circling towards, squawking at my faults

But before it makes its final swoop, it halts

What was once painful! Now seems calming.

Sheltered from what was once, constant bombing

The feeling, which seemed almost too great to bare

Will allow me to move on,

Even though it won't compare

Gone too soon

Innocent youth bestowed in the ground
As the parents stand with friends around
Wasted life now apparent and seen
Children's battles with their inner fiend
Left abruptly as though a passing train
Causing others the strenuous pain
A thought everyone's seems to keep
Continuously arising when in too deep
Witnessed now, it strains my soul
How I could have easily have taken on that role
A journey with an abrupt end Seen now as they bury my friend

Debate

The thoughts circulating cannot be controlled,
For they seem lost, they are not normal.
If sanity is material, it is something I haven't attained,
For every time I creep into arms reach, I am restrained.
A child, lost in the dark alleys of the streets,
A loner, a unique one with no similar streaks.
For my wicked imagination, lonely I belong,
An orphan of my own mind, one that's gone.
Once ordinary, but somehow wandered too deep,
On the edge, waiting for the leap,
But no courage, no drive to end.
Even though this is the last letter I will send

The Hit

Listen, your conscience is calling

Watch, the rivers from my eyes are falling

Feel, the goose bumps are rising

But remember, reality is lying

You crave it, the feeling

But it wants your soul, it's deceiving

Fetal, on the floor searching for remains

Amongst the carpet, riddled with stains

A house barren, a home no more

I picked out the insects from my sore

All over my body, overcome by itch

Battling against the fiend, this evil bitch

Devils own, in a tempting flesh

The blood milk I crave, trading all I possess

I hunched over, feel it suppress

My feelings go numb, I stumble into rest

Decisions

Onward and forward through the demise

Observing feelings mature to size

Through the darkened alley, memories reflecting on the brick

Having my heart sink to stomach, becoming grossly sick

Through the intersection, knowing I must carry on

Smile on my face, scars on my arm

Having your future stolen, by whisper from a wench

Calmly destroying your heart in violent thrusts

Dagger to soul, blade riddled with blood

Black as tar, once rose red

Departure

Awaken all. The lonely souls

The curse to hold

The fire to scald

The darkness to tremble

The memories to assemble

Fall to peace. The wicked hearts

The grave to want

The gods to taunt

The family to grieve

The pain to leave

Today

Forgive me today, for my heart is full of sorrow

Forgive me today, cause I wont last till tomorrow

Reminisce of me today, before the memories begin to sour

Reminisce of me today, cause the hatred will soon overpower

Grieve for me today, as the casket begins to descend

Grieve for me today, for the guilt will quickly end

Forget me today, as the dreams constantly follow

Forget me today, till your heart becomes hallow

Love me today, for tomorrow it's not expected

Love me today, before the idea becomes infected

Printed in the United States
By Bookmasters